The Constitution of
The State of Connecticut
A Quick Reference Guide

Bootblack Budget Books
Copyright 2018 ©
ISBN-13: 978-1985796102
ISBN-10: 1985796104

Contents:

Preamble – Page 03

Article I: Declaration of Rights – Page 04

Article II: Of the Distribution of Powers – Page 08

Article III: Of the Legislative Department – Page 09

Article IV: Of the Executive Department – Page 16

Article V: Of the Judicial Department – Page 24

Article VI: Of the Qualifications of the Electors – Page 26

Article VII: Of Religion – Page 29

Article VIII: Of Education – Page 30

Article XIX: Of Impeachments – Page 31

Article X: Of Home Rule – Page 32

Article XI: General Provisions – Page 33

Article XII: Of Amendments to the Constitution – Page 35

Article XIII: Of Constitutional Conventions – Page 36

Article XIV: The Effective Date of this Constitution – Page 38

PREAMBLE

The People of Connecticut acknowledging with gratitude, the good providence of God, in having permitted them to enjoy a free government; do, in order more effectually to define, secure, and perpetuate the liberties, rights and privileges which they have derived from their ancestors; hereby, after a careful consideration and revision, ordain and establish the following constitution and form of civil government.

ARTICLE I: DECLARATION OF RIGHTS

Section 1. All men when they form a social compact, are equal in rights; and no man or set of men are entitled to exclusive public emoluments or privileges from the community.

Section 2. All political power is inherent in the people, and all free governments are founded on their authority, and instituted for their benefit; and they have at all times an undeniable and indefeasible right to alter their form of government in such manner as they may think expedient.

Section 3. The exercise and enjoyment of religious profession and worship, without discrimination, shall forever be free to all persons in the state; provided, that the right hereby declared and established, shall not be so construed as to excuse acts of licentiousness, or to justify practices inconsistent with the peace and safety of the state.

Section 4. Every citizen may freely speak, write and publish his sentiments on all subjects, being responsible for the abuse of that liberty.

Section 5. No law shall ever be passed to curtail or restrain the liberty of speech or of the press.

Section 6. In all prosecutions or indictments for libels, the truth may be given in evidence, and the jury shall have the right to determine the law and the facts, under the direction of the court.

Section 7. The people shall be secure in their persons, houses, papers and possessions from unreasonable searches or seizures; and no warrant to search any place, or to seize any person or things, shall issue without describing them as nearly as may be, nor without probable cause supported by oath or affirmation.

Section 8. In all criminal prosecutions, the accused shall have a right to be heard by himself and by counsel; to be informed of the nature and cause of the accusation; to be confronted by the witnesses against him; to have compulsory process to obtain witnesses in his behalf; to be released on bail upon sufficient security, except in capital offenses, where the proof is evident or the presumption great; and in all prosecutions by indictment or information, to a speedy, public trial by an impartial jury. No person shall be compelled to give evidence against himself, nor be deprived of life, liberty or property without due process of law, nor shall excessive bail be required nor excessive fines imposed. No person shall be held to answer for any crime, punishable by death or life imprisonment, unless on a presentment or an indictment of a grand jury, except in the armed forces, or in the militia when in actual service in time of war or public danger.

Section 9. No person shall be arrested, detained or punished, except in cases clearly warranted by law.

Section 10. All courts shall be open, and every person, for an injury done to him in his person, property or reputation, shall have remedy by due course of law, and right and justice administered without sale, denial or delay.

Section 11. The property of no person shall be taken for public use, without just compensation therefor.

Section 12. The privileges of the writ of habeas corpus shall not be suspended, unless, when in case of rebellion or invasion, the public safety may require it; nor in any case, but by the legislature.

Section 13. No person shall be attainted of treason or felony, by the legislature.

Section 14. The citizens have a right, in a peaceable manner, to assemble for their common good, and to apply to those invested with the powers of government, for redress of grievances, or other proper purposes, by petition, address or remonstrance.

Section 15. Every citizen has a right to bear arms in defense of himself and the state.

Section 16. The military shall, in all cases, and at all times, be in strict subordination to the civil power.

Section 17. No soldier shall, in time of peace, be quartered in any house, without the consent of the owner; nor in time of war, but in a manner to be prescribed by law.

Section 18. No hereditary emoluments, privileges or honors, shall ever be granted, or conferred in this state.

Section 19. The right of trial by jury shall remain inviolate.

Section 20. No person shall be denied the equal protection of the law nor be subjected to segregation or discrimination in the exercise or enjoyment of his civil or political rights because of religion, race, color, ancestry or national origin.

ARTICLE II: OF THE DISTRIBUTION OF POWERS

Section 1. The powers of government shall be divided into three distinct departments, and each of them confided to a separate magistracy, to wit, those which are legislative, to one; those which are executive, to another; and those which are judicial, to another.

ARTICLE III: OF THE LEGISLATIVE DEPARTMENT

Section 1. The legislative power of the state shall be vested in two distinct houses or branches; the one to be styled the senate, the other the house of representatives, and both together the general assembly. The style of their laws shall be: Be it enacted by the Senate and House of Representatives in General Assembly convened.

Section 2. There shall be a regular session of the general assembly to commence on the Wednesday following the first Monday of the January next succeeding the election of its members, and at such other times as the general assembly shall judge necessary; but the person administering the office of governor may, on special emergencies, convene the general assembly at any other time. All regular and special sessions of the general assembly shall be held at Hartford, but the person administering the office of governor may, in case of special emergency, convene the assembly at any other place in the state. The general assembly shall adjourn each regular session not later than the first Wednesday after the first Monday in June following its organization and shall adjourn each special session upon completion of its business. If any bill passed by any regular or special session or any appropriation item described in Section 16 of Article IV has been disapproved by the governor prior to its adjournment, and has not been reconsidered by the assembly, or is so disapproved after such adjournment, the secretary of the state shall reconvene the general assembly on the second Monday after the last day on which the governor is authorized to transmit or has transmitted every bill to the secretary with his objections pursuant to Section 15 of Article IV of this constitution, whichever occurs first;

provided if such Monday falls on a legal holiday the general assembly shall be reconvened on the next following day. The reconvened session shall be for the sole purpose of reconsidering and, if the assembly so desires, repassing such bills. The general assembly shall adjourn sine die not later than three days following its reconvening.

Section 3. The senate shall consist of not less than thirty and not more than fifty members, each of whom shall be an elector residing in the senatorial district from which he is elected. Each senatorial district shall be contiguous as to territory and shall elect no more than one senator.

Section 4. The house of representatives shall consist of not less than one hundred twenty-five and not more than two hundred twenty-five members, each of whom shall be an elector residing in the assembly district from which he is elected. Each assembly district shall be contiguous as to territory and shall elect no more than one representative. For the purpose of forming assembly districts no town shall be divided except for the purpose of forming assembly districts wholly within the town.

Section 5. The establishment of districts in the general assembly shall be consistent with federal constitutional standards.

Section 6. a. The assembly and senatorial districts as now established by law shall continue until the regular session of the general assembly next after the completion of the next census of the United States . Such general assembly shall, upon roll call, by a yea vote of at least two-thirds of the membership of each house, enact such plan of districting as is necessary to preserve a proper apportionment of representation in accordance with the principles recited in this article. Thereafter the general assembly shall decennially at its next regular session following the completion of the census of the United States, upon roll call, by a yea vote of at least two-thirds of the membership of each house, enact such plan of districting as is necessary in accordance with the provisions of this article.

b. If the general assembly fails to enact a plan of districting by the first day of the April next following the completion of the decennial census of the United States, the governor shall forthwith appoint a commission consisting of the eight members designated by the president pro tempore of the senate, the speaker of the house of representatives, the minority leader of the senate and the minority leader of the house of representatives, each of whom shall designate two members of the commission, provided that there are members of no more than two political parties in either the senate or the house of representatives. In the event that there are members of more than two political parties in a house of the general assembly, all members of that house belonging to the parties other than that of the president pro tempore of the senate or the speaker of the house of representatives, as the case may be, shall select one of their number, who shall designate two members of the commission in lieu of the designation by the minority leader of that house.

c. The commission shall proceed to consider the alteration of districts in accordance with the principles recited in this article and it shall submit a plan of districting to the secretary of the state by the first day of the July next succeeding the appointment of its members. No plan shall be submitted to the secretary unless it is certified by at least six members of the commission. Upon receiving such plan the secretary shall publish the same forthwith, and, upon publication, such plan of districting shall have the full force of law.

d. If by the first day of the July next succeeding the appointment of its members the commission fails to submit a plan of districting, a board of three persons shall forthwith be empaneled. The speaker of the house of representatives and the minority leader of the house of representatives shall each designate, as one member of the board, a judge of the superior court of the state, provided that there are members of no more than two political parties in the house of representatives. In the event that there are members of more than two political parties in the house of representatives, all members belonging to the parties other than that of the speaker shall select one of their number, who shall then designate, as one member of the board, a judge of the superior court of the state, in lieu of the designation by the minority leader of the house of representatives. The two members of the board so designated shall select an elector of the state as the third member.

e. The board shall proceed to consider the alteration of districts in accordance with the principles recited in this article and shall, by the first day of the October next succeeding its selection, submit a plan of districting to the secretary. No plan shall be submitted to the secretary unless it is certified by at least two members of the board. Upon receiving such plan, the secretary shall publish the same forthwith, and, upon publication, such plan of districting shall have full force of law.

Section 7. The treasurer, secretary of the state, and comptroller shall canvass publicly the votes for senators and representatives. The person in each senatorial district having the greatest number of votes for senator shall be declared to be duly elected for such district, and the person in each assembly district having the greatest number of votes for representative shall be declared to be duly elected for such district. The general assembly shall provide by law the manner in which an equal and the greatest number of votes for two or more persons so voted for for senator or representative shall be resolved. The return of votes, and the result of the canvass, shall be submitted to the house of representatives and to the senate on the first day of the session of the general assembly. Each house shall be the final judge of the election returns and qualifications of its own members.

Section 8. A general election for members of the general assembly shall be held on the Tuesday after the first Monday of November, biennially, in the even-numbered years. The general assembly shall have power to enact laws regulating and prescribing the order and manner of voting for such members, for filling vacancies in either the house of representatives or the senate, and providing for the election of representatives or senators at some time subsequent to the Tuesday after the first Monday of November in all cases when it shall so happen that the electors in any district shall fail on that day to elect a representative or senator.

Section 9. At all elections for members of the general assembly the presiding officers in the several towns shall receive the votes of the electors, and count and declare them in open meeting. The presiding officers shall make and certify duplicate lists of the persons voted for, and of the number of votes for each. One list shall be delivered within three days to the town clerk, and within ten days after such meeting, the other shall be delivered under seal to the secretary of the state.

Section 10. The members of the general assembly shall hold their offices from the Wednesday following the first Monday of the January next succeeding their election until the Wednesday after the first Monday of the third January next succeeding their election, and until their successors are duly qualified.

Section 11. No member of the general assembly shall, during the term for which he is elected, hold or accept any appointive position or office in the judicial or executive department of the state government, or in the courts of the political subdivisions of the state, or in the government of any county. No member of congress, no person holding any office under the authority of the United States and no person holding any office in the judicial or executive department of the state government or in the government of any county shall be a member of the general assembly during his continuance in such office.

Section 12. The house of representatives, when assembled, shall choose a speaker, clerk and other officers. The senate shall choose a president pro tempore, clerk and other officers, except the president. A majority of each house shall constitute a quorum to do business; but a smaller number may adjourn from day to day, and compel the attendance of absent members in such manner and under such penalties as each house may prescribe.

Section 13. Each house shall determine the rules of its own proceedings, and punish members for disorderly conduct, and, with the consent of two-thirds, expel a member, but not a second time for the same cause; and shall have all other powers necessary for a branch of the legislature of a free and independent state.

Section 14. Each house shall keep a journal of its proceedings, and publish the same when required by one-fifth of its members, except such parts as in the judgment of a majority require secrecy. The yeas and nays of the members of either house shall, at the desire of one-fifth of those present, be entered on the journals.

Section 15. The senators and representatives shall, in all cases of civil process, be privileged from arrest, during any session of the general assembly, and for four days before the commencement and after the termination of any session thereof. And for any speech or debate in either house, they shall not be questioned in any other place.

Section 16. The debates of each house shall be public, except on such occasions as in the opinion of the house may require secrecy.

Section 17. The salary of the members of the general assembly and the transportation expenses of its members in the performance of their legislative duties shall be determined by law.

ARTICLE IV: OF THE EXECUTIVE DEPARTMENT

Section 1. A general election for governor, lieutenant-governor, secretary of the state, treasurer and comptroller shall be held on the Tuesday after the first Monday of November, 1966, and quadrennially thereafter.

Section 2. Such officers shall hold their respective offices from the Wednesday following the first Monday of the January next succeeding their election until the Wednesday following the first Monday of the fifth January succeeding their election and until their successors are duly qualified.

Section 3. In the election of governor and lieutenant-governor, voting for such offices shall be as a unit. The name of no candidate for either office, nominated by a political party or by petition, shall appear on the voting machine ballot labels except in conjunction with the name of the candidate for the other office.

Section 4. At the meetings of the electors in the respective towns held quadrennially as herein provided for the election of state officers, the presiding officers shall receive the votes and shall count and declare the same in the presence of the electors. The presiding officers shall make and certify duplicate lists of the persons voted for, and of the number of votes for each. One list shall be delivered within three days to the town clerk, and within ten days after such meeting, the other shall be delivered under seal to the secretary of the state. The votes so delivered shall be counted, canvassed and declared by the treasurer, secretary, and comptroller, within the month of November. The vote for treasurer shall be counted, canvassed and declared by the secretary and comptroller only; the vote for secretary shall be counted, canvassed and declared by the treasurer and comptroller only; and the vote for comptroller shall be counted, canvassed and declared by the treasurer and secretary only. A fair list of the persons and number of votes given for each, together with the returns of the presiding officers, shall be, by the treasurer, secretary and comptroller, made and laid before the general assembly, then next to be held, on the first day of the session thereof. In the election of governor, lieutenant-governor, secretary, treasurer, comptroller and attorney general, the person found upon the count by the treasurer, secretary and comptroller in the manner herein provided, to be made and announced before December fifteenth of the year of the election, to have received the greatest number of votes for each of such offices, respectively, shall be elected thereto; provided, if the election of any of them shall be contested as provided by statute, and if such a contest shall proceed to final judgment, the person found by the court to have received the greatest number of votes shall be elected. If two or more persons shall be found upon the count of the treasurer, secretary and comptroller to have received an equal and the greatest number of votes for any of said offices, and the election is not contested, the general assembly on the second day of its session shall hold a joint convention of both houses, at which, without debate, a ballot shall be taken to choose such officer from those persons who received such a vote; and the balloting shall continue on that or subsequent days until one of such persons is chosen by a majority vote of those present and voting. The general assembly shall have power to enact laws regulating and prescribing the order and manner of voting for such officers. The general assembly shall by law prescribe the manner in which all questions concerning the election of a governor or lieutenant-governor shall be determined.

Section 5. The supreme executive power of the state shall be vested in the governor. No person who is not an elector of the state, and who has not arrived at the age of thirty years, shall be eligible.

Section 6. The lieutenant-governor shall possess the same qualifications as are herein prescribed for the governor.

Section 7. The compensations of the governor and lieutenant-governor shall be established by law, and shall not be varied so as to take effect until after an election, which shall next succeed the passage of the law establishing such compensations.

Section 8. The governor shall be captain general of the militia of the state, except when called into the service of the United States .

Section 9. He may require information in writing from the officers in the executive department, on any subject relating to the duties of their respective offices.

Section 10. The governor, in case of a disagreement between the two houses of the general assembly, respecting the time of adjournment, may adjourn them to such time as he shall think proper, not beyond the day of the next stated session.

Section 11. He shall, from time to time, give to the general assembly, information of the state of the government, and recommend to their consideration such measures as he shall deem expedient.

Section 12. He shall take care that the laws be faithfully executed.

Section 13. The governor shall have power to grant reprieves after conviction, in all cases except those of impeachment, until the end of the next session of the general assembly, and no longer.

Section 14. All commissions shall be in the name and by authority of the state of Connecticut; shall be sealed with the state seal, signed by the governor, and attested by the secretary of the state.

Section 15. Each bill which shall have passed both houses of the general assembly shall be presented to the governor. Bills may be presented to the governor after the adjournment of the general assembly, and the general assembly may prescribe the time and method of performing all ministerial acts necessary or incidental to the administration of this section. If the governor shall approve a bill, he shall sign and transmit it to the secretary of the state, but if he shall disapprove, he shall transmit it to the secretary with his objections, and the secretary shall thereupon return the bill with the governor's objections to the house in which it originated. After the objections shall have been entered on its journal, such house shall proceed to reconsider the bill. If, after such reconsideration, that house shall again pass it, but by the approval of at least two-thirds of its members, it shall be sent with the objections to the other house, which shall also reconsider it. If approved by at least two-thirds of the members of the second house, it shall be a law and be transmitted to the secretary; but in such case the votes of each house shall be determined by yeas and nays and the names of the members voting for and against the bill shall be entered on the journal of each house respectively. In case the governor shall not transmit the bill to the secretary, either with his approval or with his objections, within five calendar days, Sundays and legal holidays excepted, after the same shall have been presented to him, it shall be a law at the expiration of that period; except that, if the general assembly shall then have adjourned any regular or special session, the bill shall be a law unless the governor shall, within fifteen calendar days after the same has been presented to him, transmit it to the secretary with his objections, in which case it shall not be a law unless such bill is reconsidered and repassed by the general assembly by at least a two-thirds vote of the members of each house of the general assembly at the time of its reconvening.

Section 16. The governor shall have power to disapprove of any item or items of any bill making appropriations of money embracing distinct items while at the same time approving the remainder of the bill, and the part or parts of the bill so approved shall become effective and the item or items of appropriations so disapproved shall not take effect unless the same are separately reconsidered and repassed in accordance with the rules and limitations prescribed for the passage of bills over the executive veto. In all cases in which the governor shall exercise the right of disapproval hereby conferred he shall append to the bill at the time of signing it a statement of the item or items disapproved, together with his reasons for such disapproval, and transmit the bill and such appended statement to the secretary of the state. If the general assembly be then in session he shall forthwith cause a copy of such statement to be delivered to the house in which the bill originated for reconsideration of the disapproved items in conformity with the rules prescribed for legislative action in respect to bills which have received executive disapproval.

Section 17. The lieutenant-governor shall by virtue of his office, be president of the senate, and have, when in committee of the whole, a right to debate, and when the senate is equally divided, to give the casting vote.

Section 18. In case of the death, resignation, refusal to serve or removal from office of the governor, the lieutenant-governor shall, upon taking the oath of office of governor, be governor of the state until another is chosen at the next regular election for governor and is duly qualified. In case of the inability of the governor to exercise the powers and perform the duties of his office, or in case of his impeachment or of his absence from the state, the lieutenant-governor shall exercise the powers and authority and perform the duties appertaining to the office of governor until the disability is removed or, if the governor has been impeached, he is acquitted or, if absent, he has returned.

Section 19. If the lieutenant-governor succeeds to the office of governor, or if the lieutenant-governor dies, resigns, refuses to serve or is removed from office, the president pro tempore of the senate shall, upon taking the oath of office of lieutenant-governor, be lieutenant-governor of the state until another is chosen at the next regular election for lieutenant-governor and is duly qualified. Within fifteen days of the administration of such oath the senate, if the general assembly is in session, shall elect one of its members president pro tempore. In case of the inability of the lieutenant-governor to exercise the powers and perform the duties of his office or in case of his impeachment or absence from the state, the president pro tempore of the senate shall exercise the powers and authority and perform the duties appertaining to the office of lieutenant-governor until the disability is removed or, if the lieutenant-governor has been impeached, he is acquitted or, if absent, he has returned.

Section 20. If, while the general assembly is not in session, there is a vacancy in the office of president pro tempore of the senate, the secretary of the state shall within fifteen days convene the senate for the purpose of electing one of its members president pro tempore.

Section 21. If, at the time fixed for the beginning of the term of the governor, the governor-elect shall have died or shall have failed to qualify, the lieutenant-governor-elect, after taking the oath of office of lieutenant-governor, may qualify as governor, and, upon so qualifying, shall become governor. The general assembly may by law provide for the case in which neither the governor-elect nor the lieutenant-governor-elect shall have qualified, by declaring who shall, in such event, act as governor or the manner in which the person who is so to act shall be selected, and such person shall act accordingly until a governor or a lieutenant-governor shall have qualified.

Section 22. The treasurer shall receive all monies belonging to the state, and disburse the same only as he may be directed by law. He shall pay no warrant, or order for the disbursement of public money, until the same has been registered in the office of the comptroller.

Section 23. The secretary of the state shall have the safe keeping and custody of the public records and documents, and particularly of the acts, resolutions and orders of the general assembly, and record the same; and perform all such duties as shall be prescribed by law. He shall be the keeper of the seal of the state, which shall not be altered.

Section 24. The comptroller shall adjust and settle all public accounts and demands, except grants and orders of the general assembly. He shall prescribe the mode of keeping and rendering all public accounts. He shall, ex officio, be one of the auditors of the accounts of the treasurer. The general assembly may assign to him other duties in relation to his office, and to that of the treasurer, and shall prescribe the manner in which his duties shall be performed.

Section 25. Sheriffs shall be elected in the several counties, on the Tuesday after the first Monday of November, 1966, and quadrennially thereafter, for the term of four years, commencing on the first day of June following their election. They shall become bound with sufficient sureties to the treasurer of the state, for the faithful discharge of the duties of their office. They shall be removable by the general assembly. In case the sheriff of any county shall die or resign, or shall be removed from office by the general assembly, the governor may fill the vacancy occasioned thereby, until the same shall be filled by the general assembly.

Section 26. A statement of all receipts, payments, funds, and debts of the state, shall be published from time to time, in such manner and at such periods, as shall be prescribed by law.

ARTICLE V: OF THE JUDICIAL DEPARTMENT

Section 1. The judicial power of the state shall be vested in a supreme court, a superior court, and such lower courts as the general assembly shall, from time to time, ordain and establish. The powers and jurisdiction of these courts shall be defined by law.

Section 2. The judges of the supreme court and of the superior court shall, upon nomination by the governor, be appointed by the general assembly in such manner as shall by law be prescribed. They shall hold their offices for the term of eight years, but may be removed by impeachment. The governor shall also remove them on the address of two-thirds of each house of the general assembly.

Section 3. Judges of the lower courts shall, upon nomination by the governor, be appointed by the general assembly in such manner as shall by law be prescribed, for terms of four years.

Section 4. Judges of probate shall be elected by the electors residing in their respective districts on the Tuesday after the first Monday of November, 1966, and quadrennially thereafter, and shall hold office for four years from and after the Wednesday after the first Monday of the next succeeding January.

Section 5. Justices of the peace for the several towns in the state shall be elected by the electors in such towns; and the time and manner of their election, the number for each town, the period for which they shall hold their offices and their jurisdiction shall be prescribed by law.

Section 6. No judge or justice of the peace shall be eligible to hold his office after he shall arrive at the age of seventy years, except that a chief justice or judge of the supreme court, a judge of the superior court, or a judge of the court of common pleas, who has attained the age of seventy years and has become a state referee may exercise, as shall be prescribed by law, the powers of the superior court or court of common pleas on matters referred to him as a state referee.

ARTICLE VI: OF THE QUALIFICATIONS OF ELECTORS

Section 1. Every citizen of the United States who has attained the age of twenty-one years, who has resided in the town in which he offers himself to be admitted to the privileges of an elector at least six months next preceding the time he so offers himself, who is able to read in the English language any article of the constitution or any section of the statutes of the state, and who sustains a good moral character, shall, on his taking such oath as may be prescribed by law, be an elector.

Section 2. The qualifications of electors as set forth in Section 1 of this article shall be decided at such times and in such manner as may be prescribed by law.

Section 3. The general assembly shall by law prescribe the offenses on conviction of which the privileges of an elector shall be forfeited and the conditions on which and methods by which such rights may be restored.

Section 4. Laws shall be made to support the privilege of free suffrage, prescribing the manner of regulating and conducting meetings of the electors, and prohibiting, under adequate penalties, all undue influence therein, from power, bribery, tumult and other improper conduct.

Section 5. In all elections of officers of the state, or members of the general assembly, the votes of the electors shall be by ballot, either written or printed, except that voting machines or other mechanical devices for voting may be used in all elections in the state, under such regulations as may be prescribed by law. The right of secret voting shall be preserved. At every election where candidates are listed by party designation and where voting machines or other mechanical devices are used, each elector shall be able at his option to vote for candidates for office under a single party designation by operating a straight ticket device, or to vote for candidates individually after first operating a straight ticket device, or to vote for candidates individually without first operating a straight ticket device.

Section 6. At all elections of officers of the state, or members of the general assembly, the electors shall be privileged from arrest, during their attendance upon, and going to, and returning from the same, on any civil process.

Section 7. The general assembly may provide by law for voting in the choice of any officer to be elected or upon any question to be voted on at an election by qualified voters of the state who are unable to appear at the polling place on the day of election because of absence from the city or town of which they are inhabitants or because of sickness, or physical disability or because the tenets of their religion forbid secular activity.

Section 8. The general assembly may provide by law for the admission as electors in absentia of members of the armed forces, the United States merchant marine, members of religious or welfare groups or agencies attached to and serving with the armed forces and civilian employees of the United States, and the spouses and dependents of such persons.

Section 9. Any person admitted as an elector in any town shall, if he removes to another town, have the privileges of an elector in such other town after residing therein for six months. The general assembly shall prescribe by law the manner in which evidence of the admission of an elector and of the duration of his current residence shall be furnished to the town to which he removes.

Section 10. Every elector shall be eligible to any office in the state, except in cases provided for in this constitution.

ARTICLE VII: OF RELIGION

Section 1. It being the right of all men to worship the Supreme Being, the Great Creator and Preserver of the Universe, and to render that worship in a mode consistent with the dictates of their consciences, no person shall by law be compelled to join or support, nor be classed or associated with, any congregation, church or religious association. No preference shall be given by law to any religious society or denomination in the state. Each shall have and enjoy the same and equal powers, rights and privileges, and may support and maintain the ministers or teachers of its society or denomination, and may build and repair houses for public worship.

ARTICLE VIII: OF EDUCATION

Section 1. There shall always be free public elementary and secondary schools in the state. The general assembly shall implement this principle by appropriate legislation.

Section 2. The state shall maintain a system of higher education, including The University of Connecticut, which shall be dedicated to excellence in higher education. The general assembly shall determine the size, number, terms and method of appointment of the governing boards of The University of Connecticut and of such constituent units or coordinating bodies in the system as from time to time may be established.

Section 3. The charter of Yale College, as modified by agreement with the corporation thereof, in pursuance of an act of the general assembly, passed in May, 1792, is hereby confirmed.

Section 4. The fund, called the SCHOOL FUND, shall remain a perpetual fund, the interest of which shall be inviolably appropriated to the support and encouragement of the public schools throughout the state, and for the equal benefit of all the people thereof. The value and amount of said fund shall be ascertained in such manner as the general assembly may prescribe, published, and recorded in the comptroller's office; and no law shall ever be made, authorizing such fund to be diverted to any other use than the encouragement and support of public schools, among the several school societies, as justice and equity shall require.

ARTICLE XIX: OF IMPEACHMENTS

Section 1. The house of representatives shall have the sole power of impeaching.

Section 2. All impeachments shall be tried by the senate. When sitting for that purpose, they shall be on oath or affirmation. No person shall be convicted without the concurrence of at least two-thirds of the members present. When the governor is impeached, the chief justice shall preside.

Section 3. The governor, and all other executive and judicial officers, shall be liable to impeachment; but judgments in such cases shall not extend further than to removal from office, and disqualification to hold any office of honor, trust or profit under the state. The party convicted, shall, nevertheless, be liable and subject to indictment, trial and punishment according to law.

Section 4. Treason against the state shall consist only in levying war against it, or adhering to its enemies, giving them aid and comfort. No person shall be convicted of treason, unless on the testimony of at least two witnesses to the same overt act, or on confession in open court. No conviction of treason, or attainder, shall work corruption of blood, or forfeiture.

ARTICLE X: OF HOME RULE

Section 1. The general assembly shall by general law delegate such legislative authority as from time to time it deems appropriate to towns, cities and boroughs relative to the powers, organization, and form of government of such political subdivisions. The general assembly shall from time to time by general law determine the maximum terms of office of the various town, city and borough elective offices. After July 1, 1969, the general assembly shall enact no special legislation relative to the powers, organization, terms of elective offices or form of government of any single town, city or borough, except as to (a) borrowing power, (b) validating acts, and (c) formation, consolidation or dissolution of any town, city or borough, unless in the delegation of legislative authority by general law the general assembly shall have failed to prescribe the powers necessary to effect the purpose of such special legislation.

Section 2. The general assembly may prescribe the methods by which towns, cities and boroughs may establish regional governments and the methods by which towns, cities, boroughs and regional governments may enter into compacts. The general assembly shall prescribe the powers, organization, form, and method of dissolution of any government so established.

ARTICLE XI: GENERAL PROVISIONS

Section 1. Members of the general assembly, and all officers, executive and judicial, shall, before they enter on the duties of their respective offices, take the following oath or affirmation, to wit:
You do solemnly swear (or affirm, as the case may be) that you will support the constitution of the United States, and the constitution of the state of Connecticut, so long as you continue a citizen thereof; and that you will faithfully discharge, according to law, the duties of the office of...........to the best of your abilities. So help you God.

Section 2. Neither the general assembly nor any county, city, borough, town or school district shall have power to pay or grant any extra compensation to any public officer, employee, agent or servant, or increase the compensation of any public officer or employee, to take effect during the continuance in office of any person whose salary might be increased thereby, or increase the pay or compensation of any public contractor above the amount specified in the contract.

Section 3. In order to insure continuity in operation of state and local governments in a period of emergency resulting from disaster caused by enemy attack, the general assembly shall provide by law for the prompt and temporary succession to the powers and duties of all public offices, the incumbents of which may become unavailable for carrying on their powers and duties.

Section 4. Claims against the state shall be resolved in such manner as may be provided by law.

Section 5. The rights and duties of all corporations shall remain as if this constitution had not been adopted; with the exception of such regulations and restrictions as are contained in this constitution. All laws not contrary to, or inconsistent with, the provisions of this constitution shall remain in force, until they shall expire by their own limitation, or shall be altered or repealed by the general assembly, in pursuance of this constitution. The validity of all bonds, debts, contracts, as well of individuals as of bodies corporate, or the state, of all suits, actions, or rights of action, both in law and equity, shall continue as if no change had taken place. All officers filling any office by election or appointment shall continue to exercise the duties thereof, according to their respective commissions or appointments, until their offices shall have been abolished or their successors selected and qualified in accordance with this constitution or the laws enacted pursuant thereto.

ARTICLE XII:
OF AMENDMENTS TO THE CONSTITUTION

Section 1. Amendments to this constitution may be proposed by any member of the senate or house of representatives. An amendment so proposed, approved upon roll call by a yea vote of at least a majority, but by less than three-fourths, of the total membership of each house, shall be published with the laws which may have been passed at the same session and be continued to the regular session of the general assembly elected at the general election to be held on the Tuesday after the first Monday of November in the next even-numbered year. An amendment so proposed, approved upon roll call by a yea vote of at least three-fourths of the total membership of each house, or any amendment which, having been continued from the previous general assembly, is again approved upon roll call by a yea vote of at least a majority of the total membership of each house, shall, by the secretary of the state, be transmitted to the town clerk in each town in the state, whose duty it shall be to present the same to the electors thereof for their consideration at the general election to be held on the Tuesday after the first Monday of November in the next even-numbered year. If it shall appear, in a manner to be provided by law, that a majority of the electors present and voting on such amendment at such election shall have approved such amendment, the same shall be valid, to all intents and purposes, as a part of this constitution. Electors voting by absentee ballot under the provisions of the statutes shall be considered to be present and voting.

ARTICLE XIII:
OF CONSTITUTIONAL CONVENTIONS

Section 1. The general assembly may, upon roll call, by a yea vote of at least two-thirds of the total membership of each house, provide for the convening of a constitutional convention to amend or revise the constitution of the state not earlier than ten years from the date of convening any prior convention.

Section 2. The question "Shall there be a Constitutional Convention to amend or revise the Constitution of the State?" shall be submitted to all the electors of the state at the general election held on the Tuesday after the first Monday in November in the even-numbered year next succeeding the expiration of a period of twenty years from the date of convening of the last convention called to revise or amend the constitution of the state, including the Constitutional Convention of 1965, or next succeeding the expiration of a period of twenty years from the date of submission of such a question to all electors of the state, whichever date shall last occur. If a majority of the electors voting on the question shall signify "yes", the general assembly shall provide for such convention as provided in section 3 of this article.

Section 3. In providing for the convening of a constitutional convention to amend or revise the constitution of the state the general assembly shall, upon roll call, by a yea vote of at least two-thirds of the total membership of each house, prescribe by law the manner of selection of the membership of such convention, the date of convening of such convention, which shall be not later than one year from the date of the roll call vote under

Section 1 of this article or one year from the date of the election under Section 2 of this article, as the case may be, and the date for final adjournment of such convention.

Section 4. Proposals of any constitutional convention to amend or revise the constitution of the state shall be submitted to all the electors of the state not later than two months after final adjournment of the convention, either as a whole or in such parts and with such alternatives as the convention may determine. Any proposal of the convention to amend or revise the constitution of the state submitted to such electors in accordance with this section and approved by a majority of such electors voting on the question shall be valid, to all intents and purposes, as a part of this constitution. Such proposals when so approved shall take effect thirty days after the date of the vote thereon unless otherwise provided in the proposal.

ARTICLE XIV:
OF THE EFFECTIVE DATE OF THIS CONSTITUTION

Section 1. This proposed constitution, submitted by the Constitutional Convention of 1965, shall become the constitution of the state of Connecticut upon approval by the people and proclamation by the governor as provided by law.

Approved at referendum on December 14, 1965; proclaimed by the Governor as adopted on December 30, 1965.

www.ingramcontent.com/pod-product-compliance
Lightning Source LLC
Chambersburg PA
CBHW030102230526
45471CB00003B/1213